Enjoy the Fun Facts!

Bret Nicolaus

# Hooray for Minnesota Lakes!

For Minnesotans (and those who wish they *were*) of All Ages

**Paul Lowrie and Bret Nicholaus**

Authors of the bestseller *Hooray for Minnesota Winters!*

Illustrations by **Jennifer Awes**

**Warm Words Press**
a division of William Randall Publishing

Warm Words Press
a division of William Randall Publishing
P.O. Box 340, Yankton, SD 57078
www.HoorayforMinnesota.com

William Randall Publishing's authors are available for seminars and speaking engagements.
If interested please contact us at the address listed above.

ATTENTION: SCHOOLS AND BUSINESSES
William Randall Publishing's books are available at quantity discounts
with bulk purchase for educational, business, or promotional use.

For more information, contact:
William Randall Publishing, Special Sales Department,
P.O. Box 340, Yankton, SD 57078

ISBN-13: 978-0-9755801-8-9
ISBN-10: 0-9755801-8-3

Printed in Korea

First Edition: July 2008

10 9 8 7 6 5 4 3 2 1

# Hooray for Minnesota Lakes!

For Minnesotans (and those who wish they *were*) of All Ages

# BEFORE
## WE EMBARK

Let's face it: Every state has its "thing." Georgia has its three p's—peaches, peanuts, and pecans. Wisconsin has its cows, and ergo its cheese. Washington has its apples, and Florida has its sunshine (actually, many states receive more sunshine per year than the Sunshine State does, but that's another story). And Minnesota? Well, we've got our lakes. All 10,000 of them (more on that later). We may get a good deal of press for our sub-zero temperatures and our 10-month winters, but we're best known for our lakes—ahhhhhh, what a beautiful and wonderful thing to be known for!

*Hooray for Minnesota Lakes!* was written and designed as a tribute to our beloved lakes. It's also a tribute to everything else that goes with them—abundant wildlife, lazy days spent fishing, cozy cabins, family memories. And since the very root of the word *Minnesota* (mni) comes from a Dakota Indian word meaning "water," it seemed right to allow this book to feature other watery highlights of our state as well, including rivers and streams (we've got nearly 70,000 miles of them!), and even waterfalls.

Naturally, we could not possibly cover everything related to Minnesota's waters within the pages of this type of book. Instead, what we have tried to do here is offer a representative sampling of water-themed topics—one for each letter of the alphabet from A to Z. Each topic is briefly covered in a short poem; most of the poems are followed by a fact-filled paragraph, which, in sticking with the lake theme of the book, we have humorously dubbed "A Shore Thing" (on a couple of occasions, the fun facts have been replaced with quotations). Between the rhymes, the trivia, the quotes, and the hand-drawn illustrations, it is our sincere hope that both adults and children will enjoy every page while learning something, too.

In the end, *Hooray for Minnesota Lakes!* makes a remarkably strong case that even though our state itself may be "watered down," the love and affection we have for Minnesota will *never* be!

Your crew,

Paul Lowrie, Bret Nicholaus, Jennifer Awes, and Ann Lundstrom

The face of the water,
in time, became a wonderful book....
And it was not a book to be read
once and thrown aside,
for it had a new story to tell every day.

*—Mark Twain (1835-1910)*

# A SHORE THING

It is quite appropriate that we begin this book with a quote by American literary icon Mark Twain. Why? Because Mark Twain, whose real name was Samuel Langhorne Clemens, chose his pen name as a result of the time he spent as a steamboat pilot on the Mississippi River (later in the book, we'll have plenty to say about the world-famous river that begins its journey right here in Minnesota). The boat's leadsman would use a line with lead to "mark" the depth of the water and then call it out to the captain. The call of "by the mark, twain" meant that the water was two fathoms deep (one fathom equals 6 feet; *twain* is an archaic form of the word *two*), the minimum depth in which a riverboat could move safely ahead.

# "A" is for Angling,

## from boat or from *shore*;

## A day spent fishing—

## who could ask for **more**?!

We're not feeding people a line when we tell them how much we love to fish in Minnesota. We really do, and the numbers bear that out (more on bears later). We easily surpass one million fishing licenses sold per year, including residents and nonresidents, and annual expenditures on fishing in our state total around $1.5 billion. The annual harvest of panfish alone is approximately 65 million pounds, with walleye adding another 30-plus million pounds to the total. All those statistics should come as no surprise when you consider the fact that Minnesota's total water area—including wetlands—is 20,526 square miles (more than the land area of Connecticut, Massachusetts, and New Jersey combined). You can't ask for a better state if you love to fish; you can't ask for a worse state if you *are* the fish!

# "B" is for the Boundary Waters,

so wild and *free*;

As far removed from the modern world

as any place could be.

## A SHORE THING

If you truly want to get away from it all, head to the portion of Minnesota's Superior National Forest known as the Boundary Waters Canoe Area Wilderness (BWCAW). At roughly 1.3 million acres in size, the BWCAW is plenty large enough to lose yourself in, but hopefully not literally. Even if you do get lost, you certainly won't be alone—there are plenty of beavers, peregrine falcons, bald eagles, bobcats, black bears, and moose to keep you company. (Did you know that moose can dive as deep as 20 feet to find food, swim more than 10 miles without stopping, and swim three times faster than the fastest human swimmer?!) Oh, yes, the Boundary Waters is also part of the range of the largest population of wolves in the lower 48 states. Actually, the BWCAW, with its more than 1,200 miles of canoe routes, 15 hiking trails, and roughly 2,000 designated campsites, is the most visited wilderness in the United States. Still, with several thousand lakes and streams surrounded by hundreds of thousands of acres of forest, people wishing to experience peace and quiet have little trouble doing so up in the Boundary Waters.

# "C" is for Cabin,

## the getaway *place*:

### A great spot to go

### to avoid the rat race.

"How beautiful it is to do nothing,
and then to rest afterward." *—Spanish Proverb*

"If people concentrated on the really important things in life,
there'd be a shortage of fishing poles." *—Doug Larson*

"In wilderness I sense the miracle of life,
and behind it our scientific accomplishments fade to trivia." *—Charles Lindbergh*

"I only went out for a walk and finally concluded to stay out till sundown;
for going out, I found, was really going in." *—John Muir*

6

# "D" is for Ducks

and their quack-quack-*quacking*;

With 22 species,

our lakes are not lacking.

We'll deal with loons a bit later in the book, but here the spotlight is on ducks—the largest group of waterfowl in Minnesota. The 22 species of ducks that nest in or visit Minnesota each year are divided into two groups: dabblers and divers. The dabblers—which include mallards (known for their explosive takeoffs from the water), northern pintails (the long-necked, long-tailed duck), and green-winged teals (Minnesota's smallest duck)—are built with legs close to the middle of their bodies, which makes it easy for them to walk on land as well as to tip up like bobbers when eating underwater plants. The divers—including canvasbacks (large ducks that can fly up to 70 miles per hour), lesser scaups (which form huge groups up to a mile wide on large lakes during migration) and redheads (the male's call sounds like a cat's meow)—have short wings, which create less drag as they swim long distances underwater searching for food. Among all of Minnesota's divers, take the most pity on the poor ruddy duck: its legs are positioned so close to its tail that the poor thing can hardly walk!

# "E" is for Evenings

spent down by the *lake*,

Watching the sun set

and taking a **break**.

A **SHORE** THING

Thanks to the geographic location of Minnesota and the fact that we are in the central time zone, we get to enjoy long summer evenings here, even if the summer itself is all too short. During the longest days of June, when the sun has already set at 8:30 in Chicago, Illinois, we still have plenty of time left to cast a line or take a leisurely walk along the lake. Even in Eitzen, Minnesota, in the far southeastern part of the state, the late-June sun doesn't set until 8:51. Move on to Little Falls (hometown of Charles Lindbergh), in the dead center of the state, and you've got sunlight until 9:12. And way up in the northwestern Minnesota town of St. Vincent, the sun doesn't drop below the horizon until 9:37. Interestingly, you don't need to leave the central time zone to experience the latest sunset (by clock time) on the mainland of the lower 48 states—though, regrettably, you *do* need to leave Minnesota. In the far northwestern section of North Dakota, near Fortuna, the sun at the end of June stays up until shortly after 10:00 pm!

# "F" is for Freighters

docked in *Duluth*;

Some are three football fields long,

to tell you the **truth**!

## A SHORE THING

There are many freighters sailing on the Great Lakes, but there are only 13 "super freighters" afloat. All of the super freighters were built in the 1970s and early 1980s. They have names like Mesabi Miner, Indiana Harbor, and Stewart J. Cort. Each of the 13 vessels can carry at least 60,000 tons of cargo, including taconite, limestone, cement, grain, and salt (60,000 tons is equal to about 15,000 full-grown elephants).  Every one of these massive ships is 105 feet wide and at least 1,000 feet long. The longest of all, the Paul R. Tregurtha, is slightly more than 1,013 feet in length, or 338 yards (think of a walloped drive by Tiger Woods). Because of their incredible length, the super freighters are restricted to just four of the five Great Lakes; they cannot enter Lake Ontario, as the St. Lawrence Seaway locks are unable to accommodate ships over 730 feet long. But Duluth, the world's largest inland seaport, sits on the shore of Lake Superior—so at any given time you just might be lucky enough to see one of these floating behemoths if you are down by the docks of Duluth.

# "G" is for Gull Lake,

## and to be very *honest*,

## It's the site of the world's largest

## ice-fishing contest.

## A SHORE THING

We Minnesotans are crazy enough to go ice fishing in the dead of winter simply because we *can*. But offer us an ice-fishing contest where first prize is a brand-new 4X4 pickup truck, and even those who bemoan winter will eagerly show up. Every year since 1991, thousands of anglers from Minnesota—not to mention other states and other countries—have made the late-January journey to Gull Lake, just north of Brainerd. They make the trip to participate in what is billed as the world's largest ice-fishing contest, officially called the Brainerd Jaycees Ice-Fishing Extravaganza. As many as 11,000 anglers show up each year for the three-hour event, which officially commences with a cannon blast. Each angler entered in the contest can choose any one of 20,000 pre-drilled holes in the ice to call their own, with the hope that from their hole they will pull the winning fish. Though the new pickup truck goes to the person with the heaviest fish, there are 150 winners total (other prizes include new boats, underwater cameras, vacation packages, and gift cards, to name just a few). All proceeds from the event go to local charities, and in one recent year as much as $250,000 was raised for good causes.

# "H" is for Hot,

which it can get in the *summer*;

If you're not near a lake,

it can be a real **bummer**!

## A SHORE THING

For non-Minnesotans, putting the words HOT and MINNESOTA together makes about as much sense as putting the words FREEZING and FLORIDA together. But residents of our state understand that while we might be known for our brutal winters, we can bring the heat with the best of them. For example, the all-time record-high temperature in Minnesota is 114 degrees, set on July 29, 1917, in Beardsley, and tied on July 6, 1936, in Moorhead. Also in the summer of 1936, the Twin Cities experienced a record 14 straight days where the temperature reached or exceeded 100 degrees! (In a truly ironic comparison, Miami, Florida, has *never* recorded a temperature higher than 100 degrees.) Curious about the official all-time high temperature for International Falls? Well, in June of 1995, the "Icebox of the Nation" hit 99 degrees. But here's the most staggering statistic of all: On July 30, 1999, Red Wing, Minnesota, had an air temperature of 97 degrees along with a dew point of 84. That translated into a heat index of 125 sweltering degrees, the highest in the history of Minnesota weather records. Even the cold summertime waters of Lake Superior would have felt invigorating on *that* day!

# "I" is for Itching

from head to *toe*;

Minnesota's mosquitoes will getcha,

ya know!

## A SHORE THING

Mosquitoes—now there's a fun topic for you. While some of you may be wishing we had scratched this topic from our list of options for the letter "I," we just couldn't do a book about Minnesota's lakes without including something on our "state bird"—the mosquito. The next time you're itching to head out to the lake, keep a few facts in mind: There are roughly 50 species of mosquitoes in Minnesota, and about 30 of them bite humans. Only female mosquitoes bite, and they do so because they require a blood meal to help develop their fertile eggs (a single meal will nourish 100 eggs or more). Since one meal at your expense can literally double the weight of the female mosquito, she often times cannot fly away after eating. If she does manage to get away with the goods before a swift slap sends her to mosquito nirvana, she will only bite one or two more times in her lifetime (most mosquitoes only live two to four weeks beyond the pupa stage). If the whole biting thing drives you crazy in the summertime, you'll just have to stop giving off body heat and exhaling carbon dioxide; mosquitoes fly in for the feeding when they detect either of those two things!

# "J" is for Johnboat,

a skiff you can *take*

Into hard-to-reach places

out on the lake.

## A SHORE THING

Johnboats, fishing boats, pontoon boats, kayaks, canoes, personal watercraft, yachts—there's a boat for everyone and every purpose, and nowhere in the United States will you find more boats per capita than in Minnesota. A recent statewide count of boats revealed more than 850,000 registered boats—one for every six men, women, and children in the state. Besides being number one in the nation in terms of boats per capita, there are only three states that beat us in outright boat registrations, and those are the far more populous states of California, Florida, and Michigan. Although the total number of boats in Minnesota has risen about 30% in the last two decades, using boats for fishing is on the decline; surveys have indicated that pleasure boating is now the most popular use for boats in our state. But whether we boat to fish or just to have fun, it's safe to say that Minnesotans are most content when they are on the water.

# "K" is for Kids,

splishing and *splashing*;

And running and jumping

and smiling and laughing.

"We've had bad luck with our kids—they've all grown up!" —*Christopher Morley*

"The real trouble with the world is that too many people grow up....
They don't remember what it's like to be 12 years old." —*Walt Disney*

"The average child laughs about 400 times per day,
but the average adult laughs only 15 times per day.
What happened to the other 385 laughs?" —*Source unknown*

# "L" is for Loon,

## our distinctive state *bird*;

## Its call is as haunting

## as anything you've heard.

# A SHORE THING

Hoot, Tremolo, Yodel, and Wail. No, it's not the name of some upstart law firm in Minneapolis, it's the four unique sounds that the common loon makes. The hoot is a short call often used to communicate among parents and young; the tremolo (also known as the loon laugh) means the bird is excited or alarmed; the loud yodel sound is made only by the male when guarding his territory during breeding season (each male loon has its own signature yodel, which can be heard as far as a mile away); and the long, haunting wail allows a loon to figure out where it is relative to other loons. Perhaps their other-worldly sounds shouldn't surprise us; after all, the loon has been around for about 50 million years, making it the oldest and most primitive living bird. A few other facts about these extremely shy creatures:

- ◊ Minnesota has roughly 12,000 loons (more than any other state except Alaska)
- ◊ A loon can dive as deep as 250 feet to search for food
- ◊ Loons can fly at speeds in excess of 75 miles per hour
- ◊ The red that you see in the loon's eyes enables it to see underwater
- ◊ The loon's body contains solid bones; most birds' bones are hollow and light

# "M" is for the Mighty Mississippi—

of course, it's not a *lake*;

But it's known throughout the world,

and it begins in OUR state!

## A SHORE THING

The Mississippi River is, without question, the most famous river in the United States. From beginning to end, the world's 14th longest river touches 10 states and millions of lives. The renowned historian Stephen E. Ambrose has written that the Mississippi River is "both the spiritual heart and economic backbone of our country." Considering that statement, we should be mighty proud to think that this mighty river begins in our own backyard. The true source of the river, which had been sought for many years, was finally discovered in 1832 by historian Henry Rowe Schoolcraft: The source was Lake Itasca (the famous explorer Zebulon Pike had, years earlier, misidentified the source as Leech Lake). Today, visitors to the 32,000-acre Itasca State Park (Minnesota's oldest state park) can experience the thrill of stepping across the Mississippi River, which begins as a seemingly insignificant trickle over some stones. At the headwaters, the river is crystal clear, actually heading due north for about 15 miles before turning east and then gradually beginning the long journey south (the first 680 miles flow through Minnesota, nearly 29% of the river's total distance). By the time the 2,352-mile-long Father of Waters reaches the Gulf of Mexico, where it discharges as much as 700,000 cubic feet of murky water per second, it has definitely earned another of its many nicknames: Big Muddy.

# "N" is for No,

as in no lakes *around*;

In four of our counties,

no lakes can be found.

A **SHORE** THING

In our lake-laden state, it's hard to imagine that there could be a single county without at least one natural lake in it. But, alas, there are actually *four* Minnesota counties with no natural lakes (as opposed to man-made impoundments or wetlands) within their borders: Mower (on the Iowa border), Olmsted (which includes the city of Rochester), Pipestone (on the South Dakota border, and just north of Rock County), and Rock (the most southwestern county in our state). Then again, with 87 total counties in our state, that means that 95% of our counties *do* have at least one natural lake in them. The Minnesota county with the most lakes and wetlands? Otter Tail (which, for a point of reference, includes the town of Fergus Falls), with 1,534.

29

# "O" is for One hundred and fifty-eight *fish*,

## The number of fish

## on our official fish list.

A SHORE THING

There's a good reason why so many world-class anglers have adopted Minnesota as their home: the fishing in our state is absolutely fin-tastic! With 158 species of fish in our waters, you'll never run out of reasons to drop a line or two. With the right bait, a little patience, and a lot of luck, you just might land the hard-to-catch muskie, aka "the fish of 1,000 casts"; or a northern pike, well known for its explosive aerial acrobats; or a largemouth bass, whose mouth is so big it could easily swallow its own head. If you're into fly fishing, you'd probably love to catch a beautiful brown trout in one of our streams. And if you're like the majority of Minnesotans, you long to catch our state fish—the walleye. From the lake sturgeon (our state's largest fish) to the eelpout (it gets its own festival in Walker), from the yellow bullhead (beware those stabbing spines!) to the bigmouth buffalo (what a cool name for a fish!), Minnesotans have 158 reasons to be fin-atical about fishing!

# "P" is for Portaging

miles of *ground*;

The word *portage* can serve

both as verb and as noun.

## A SHORE THING

Anyone who has spent even a short amount of time in northern Minnesota, with its endless lakes and pristine forests, is likely familiar with the term *portage*. It's one of those odd words that can be used either as a noun or a verb (like the word *fish*). When used as a verb, portage refers to the practice of carrying a canoe or other type of boat over land in order to avoid an obstacle on the waterway, such as a waterfall or swirling rapids. You would also portage if you were trying to go from one body of water to another and the two were separated by land. This is where it gets a little complicated: the land and/or trail on which you portage (the verb) is called a portage (the noun). The person doing the portaging on the portage is called a porter. In days gone by, places where porters did their portaging sometimes became permanent settlements, and they frequently kept the word *portage* in the name, e.g., Grand Portage, Minnesota. Now, proud as we are, we might be inclined to believe that portaging got its start right here in Minnesota (didn't everything?!). Sadly, that's not the case. History records show that a paved trackway called the Diolkos existed in Ancient Greece. Its purpose was to enable boats to be moved across the Isthmus of Corinth, from the Gulf of Corinth to the Saronic Gulf.

33

# "Q" is for Quiet,

which High Falls is *not*:

There's plenty of noise

with its 120-foot drop!

## A SHORE THING

Minnesota may not have a significantly large quantity of waterfalls, but the height of one of our falls more than makes up for it. Head to the town of Grand Portage, Minnesota, and then proceed just a few more miles to the U.S./Canadian border. That's where you'll see—and certainly hear—the High Falls of the Pigeon River, also known as Pigeon Falls. The 120-foot thunderous plunge makes High Falls the highest waterfall in our state. Thanks to a half-mile trail and boardwalk that lead to an overlook area, it's easy to view the awe-inspiring cascade located within Grand Portage State Park. But before we start feeling too smug about the height of High Falls, let's keep it in perspective: The tallest officially measured waterfall in the U.S. is California's Yosemite Falls, which has a vertical drop of 2,425 feet; the world's tallest waterfall is Venezuela's Angel Falls, with a total plunge of 3,230 feet!

# "R" is for Record,

## as in record-sized *fish*;

## If someone tells you they caught one,

## just answer, "You wish!"

# A SHORE THING

The fishing trip might be over, but that means the fish stories are just about to begin. If you live in Minnesota, you know the routine. As the years pass, the once good-sized fish you caught becomes enormous, and the enormous fish might even end up record-sized. Far more likely than claiming you hauled in a trophy fish is telling of "the big one that got away." But once in a blue moon, the fish story is actually true. On the rarest of rare occasions, the big one *doesn't* get away. Listed below are just a few of the amazing-but-true record-sized fish caught in Minnesota waters (listed by species, weight, where caught, and year):

- Largemouth Bass/8 lbs. 15 oz./Auburn Lake/2005
- Walleye/17 lbs. 8 oz./Seagull River/1979
- Bigmouth Buffalo/41 lbs. 11 oz./Mississippi River/1991
- Lake Trout/43 lbs. 8 oz./Lake Superior/1955
- Northern Pike/45 lbs. 12 oz./Basswood Lake/1929
- Lake Sturgeon/94 lbs. 4 oz./Kettle River/1994

# "S" is for Superior,

## our greatest lake by *far*;

## Among the five Great Lakes,

## it really is the star.

## A SHORE THING

From Duluth to Grand Portage, the cold, wind-driven, often dangerous water of Lake Superior (case in point, the 1975 shipwreck of the Edmund Fitzgerald) crashes into Minnesota's rugged shores. In total, Lake Superior has a surface area of 31,700 square miles, contains 2,904 cubic miles of water (about three quadrillion gallons), and reaches a depth of 1,333 feet—easily beating out the other four Great Lakes in each of those categories. In fact, Superior contains as much water as the other four Great Lakes combined, with two extra Lake Eries thrown in. Lake Superior is the world's largest freshwater lake in terms of surface area (Minnesota can claim about 1,500 square miles of it), but the greatest Great Lake can't claim the top spot in every category. Oregon's Crater Lake is actually the deepest lake in the U.S., at 1,932 feet deep. Russia's Lake Baikal is the world's deepest lake (it happens to be freshwater), with a maximum depth of 5,314 feet; it is also the world's largest freshwater lake in terms of volume, with 5,521 cubic miles of water (roughly equal to the volume of all five North American Great Lakes combined!). Finally, the world's largest non-freshwater lake both by surface area and volume is the salty Caspian Sea: It has a surface area of 143,200 square miles and contains 18,900 cubic miles of water.

# "T" is for Ten Thousand,

the number on our *plate*;

The real total,

however, is up for debate.

## A SHORE THING

10,000 is a nice, round number—easy to remember, and therefore a great way for Minnesota to promote itself to the other 49 states. But as almost every Minnesotan knows, it's not the *real* number of lakes in our state. So how many lakes do we actually have? According to the Minnesota Department of Natural Resources, there are 11,842 lakes throughout the state; but to be included in this "official" count, a lake must be 10 acres or larger in size (a size large enough to produce a wave-swept shore). Some sources outside the DNR claim around 15,000 lakes for our state, but that presumably includes lakes *less* than 10 acres in size. In addition to our lakes, we also have slightly more than 9,700 documented wetlands. Lakes and wetlands in Minnesota are lumped into a category called Public Waters; the wetlands and lakes Public Waters total is 21,561 (the number is even higher if you include public waters watercourses). So our license plate says 10,000 lakes, the official number is 11,842, some sources claim around 15,000, and 21,561 is the number if wetlands are included with lakes (and not everyone agrees on what constitutes a wetland and what constitutes a lake). It's all way too complicated—let's just say we have a LOT of water and move on to letter "U."

# "U" is for Upper,

one half of *Red Lake*;

To leave out the Lower

would be a mistake.

## A SHORE THING

Even a non-Minnesotan would have no trouble locating Red Lake on a map of Minnesota. North of Bemidji, south of Baudette, it practically jumps off the page because of its size. When taking into account all lakes where the entire body of water lies within the borders of Minnesota, Red Lake is our largest by far: slightly more than 444 square miles, or 284,264 acres (Mille Lacs comes in second at 132,516 acres, Leech Lake third at 111,527 acres). Although uninterrupted by any land, Red Lake is made up of two lakes—Upper Red and Lower Red. Upper Red Lake is 119,274 acres in size; Lower Red Lake is larger at 164,990 acres. If it weren't for the lower lake, Red Lake would be much smaller in size (though still quite formidable, of course). Thankfully, the two are considered one, giving us a body of water more than worthy of our best boating, er, boasting. *(Note: By comparison, Wisconsin's largest lake, Winnebago, is 137,708 acres.)*

# "V" is for Vermilion,

a lake with a lot of *shore*;

In fact, in Minnesota,

no other lake has more!

A **SHORE** THING

If you decided to jump in your car and take a trip from Minneapolis, Minnesota, to Des Moines, Iowa (though we're not quite sure what would possess you to do that), it would require that you travel 243 miles. By comparison, to go from Duluth, Minnesota, to Fargo, North Dakota, you would need to cruise clear across the state for 258 miles. And the distance (as the car drives, not as the crow flies) from St. Paul, Minnesota, to Sioux Falls, South Dakota, is 272 miles. Yet, incredibly, not a single one of these trips is as long in terms of miles as the shoreline of Lake Vermilion, located near the Mesabi and Vermilion Iron Ranges. With 290 miles of twisting and turning shoreline, Lake Vermilion grabs the top spot in Minnesota for the "length of shoreline" category; even as the crow flies, it's 27 miles from the east end of the lake to the west end. Suffice it to say, there's no such thing as a leisurely walk around Lake Vermilion.

# "W" is for Wetlands,

and Wild Rice, *too*;

Waterskiing was born on Lake Pepin—

it's true!

## A SHORE THING

♦ Minnesota has approximately 10 million acres of wetlands (one hundred years ago, more than 20 million wetland acres covered the state). A wetland has standing water or saturated soil for at least a portion of the growing season and is covered with plants that have adapted to wet conditions.

♦ Wild rice, the only cereal grain native to North America, is still to this day hand-harvested by Native Americans along the edges of shallow lakes and streams in northern Minnesota. Wild rice is also cultivated and then harvested using large, modified grain combines in drained paddies. Minnesota is one of the world's largest producers of cultivated wild rice, harvesting 4 to 6 million pounds per year.

♦ In the summer of 1922, an 18-year-old Minnesotan named Ralph Samuelson invented water skiing on Lake Pepin (a wide portion of the Mississippi River between Minnesota and Wisconsin). Known as "The Father of Water Skiing," Samuelson also performed the first ski jump on water in the summer of 1925.

# "X" is for Extremely,

## as in extremely *deep*—

## Like the depth of Embarrass Mine Pit,

## at 472 feet!

A **SHORE** THING

There are deep lakes, and then there are deeeeeeeeep lakes. At a depth of 472 feet, the Embarrass Mine Pit, known locally as Lake Mine, is believed to be the deepest inland lake in our state. This 156-acre artificial lake, near Embarrass, Minnesota, was once an iron-ore mine; when mining ceased in 1977 and the water pumps stopped pumping, the pit filled with crystal-clear water and fish were stocked over time—making the lake ideal for snorkeling and scuba diving. Many other abandoned mining pits in this part of the state are filled with water and fish today, and the formerly desolate landscape is now a beautiful place to visit.

The deepest *natural* lake in Minnesota can be found up in the Arrowhead: it's Saganaga Lake (which we share with Canada), at 240 feet deep. The deepest natural lake completely within the borders of Minnesota is Gabimichigami Lake, in Cook County, at 226 feet deep.

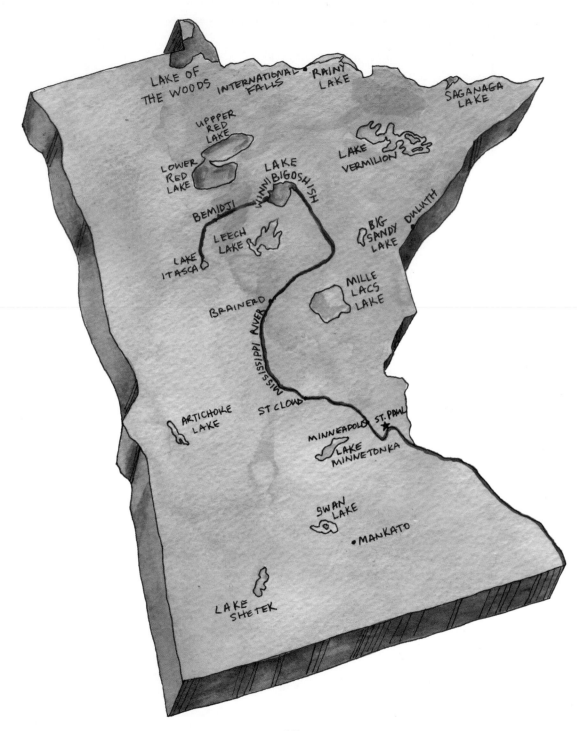

# "Y" is for Yearning

## for summer *vacation*,

## When Lake Whatchamacallit

## is our destination.

# A SHORE THING

It's the dead of winter in Minnesota. The mercury hasn't topped 32 degrees in more than six weeks. The days are short and the nights are long. The snow's piling up and you're feeling down. Then, suddenly, you have a thought that warms your soul: You're soaking up the sun as you sit on the dock with your feet dangling in the water, or perhaps as you zip across the water in your boat. But what lake are you on? There's a good chance you're on Mud Lake, the most common lake name in Minnesota (there are 224 Mud Lakes among us). Maybe you're on one of the many famous lakes—Cass, Leech, Mille Lacs, Pelican, Winnibigoshish. If you like straddling the U.S./Canadian border, Lake of the Woods, Rainy Lake, or Saganaga Lake are all good possibilities. In the Twin Cities, lakes like Calhoun, Minnetonka, and White Bear await. Throughout the state, Green, Red, and Silver are options, but so are Goose, Moose, and Skunk. And let's not overlook Artichoke, Potato, and Squash—and many thousands more! Whichever lake you like to call your own, you can be certain it will be ready to greet you when summer finally arrives and the thaw is complete. For now, back to that snow blowing!

"Z" is for the Zest

we have for our *state*—

We know that it's special,

we know that it's **great**.

And a wonderful reason to love it,

we *claim*,

Is because of the lakes

that have brought us our **fame**!

A lake is the landscape's
most beautiful and expressive feature.
It is earth's eye, looking into which
the beholder measures
the depth of his own nature.

—Henry David Thoreau (1817-1862)

# THREE **EASY-TO-FOLLOW**
## SETS OF INSTRUCTIONS
### FOR NON-MINNESOTANS

**How to watch a sunset on the lake:**

1. Find out what time the sun sets.

2. Find a peaceful place to stand or sit along the shore at sunset.

3. Convince yourself that never before has the world seen a sunset as gorgeous as this one.

**How to jump off a dock:**

1. Make sure the water is deep enough to make a safe jump.

2. Walk to the edge of the dock, bend knees, and lunge forward.

3. Make a really big deal about how cold the water is.

**How to tell a fish story:**

1. Begin every morning by doing horizontal arm stretches.

2. As your reach increases over time, continue to push yourself to stretch farther.

3. Know that this is the only exercise you'll ever need to do to be a good fisherman.

# WORDS
## OF THANKS & CREDITS

When writing a book packed with statistics, there is always plenty of research and fact-checking involved. This book was no exception. Much of the time, when consulting multiple sources regarding a given statistic or story, the sources agreed with each other; that made our job easy. Occasionally, however, sources were not consistent in their reporting of the data; in those cases, we had to make an educated decision regarding which source or sources to use, and we apologize if any information in this book is found to be incorrect. Often, though not always, we used as our final authority the kind and helpful people at the Minnesota Department of Natural Resources—a huge "thank you" is due to them for answering our sometimes difficult and time-consuming questions. Their comprehensive website, dnr.state.mn.us, was also extremely helpful in our research.

Dozens of other individuals, organizations, books, magazines, and websites were also consulted in our research efforts. We would especially like to recognize the following: Explore Minnesota Tourism (not only is their staff extremely helpful, but they have a marvelous website at exploreminnesota.com), Minnesota Board of Water & Soil Resources, Minnesota Climatology Office, Grand Portage State Park, Lake Itasca State Park, *Locks & Ships, Volume Three* (made available through the Soo Locks Boat Tours), *Loon Magic for Kids* by Tom Klein, *The Mississippi and the Making of a Nation* by Stephen E. Ambrose and Douglas G. Brinkley, *Lake Country Journal Magazine, 2008 Rand McNally Road Atlas*, Brainerd Jaycees, bwcaw.org, geology.com, wcco.com, and weather.com. Also, special thanks to Richard Albright for proofreading the manuscript.

Finally, and perhaps most importantly, we would like to thank the glaciers from the last Ice Age—without their help, a book on Minnesota lakes would not have been possible.

# ABOUT THE AUTHORS

**PAUL LOWRIE** was born in St. Louis Park, Minnesota. His family moved to South Dakota when he was 10, but Lowrie returned to his home state to attend Bethel University. Since graduating with a degree in marketing in 1991, he has lived and worked in both Minnesota and South Dakota.

**BRET NICHOLAUS** is also a 1991 graduate of Bethel University, where he received his degree in communication. He has been writing professionally since 1992. Though Nicholaus is proud to say that Minnesota is his favorite state, he, his wife, and their two young boys live in his home state of Illinois. They visit Minnesota as often as they can.

# ABOUT THE DESIGNER

**ANN LUNDSTROM** was born and raised in Sioux Falls, South Dakota. Since graduating from the University of South Dakota in 2004 with a degree in graphics and multimedia, she has poured her creative energies into growing her graphic and web design business. Ann, her husband, and their twin son and daughter live in Hawarden, Iowa. The Lundstroms frequently visit family in the Minneapolis/St. Paul area.

# ABOUT
## THE ILLUSTRATOR

**JENNIFER AWES** grew up in northwestern Wisconsin, but moved to Minnesota to attend Bethel University, from which she graduated in 2003 with a theater arts degree. She and her husband, a native of Minnesota, recently moved to Connecticut, where Jennifer is studying visual art and religion at Yale University, Institute of Sacred Music.